Green Finger Fun

words and pictures by Althea

Published by Dinosaur Publications

Indoor gardening is fun and need not be expensive. Carrot tops grow into pretty ferns. Acorns and fruit pips or stones can start to grow into small trees.

You can grow plants from cuttings taken from other house plants. Spring and summer is the best time to start new plants, but many will grow at other times of year too.

Cut off the leaves and stand the carrot top in water After a few days a green fern will start to grow.

A kitchen spoon and fork
make good gardening tools.
A plastic bag over a pot makes
a little self-watering greenhouse.
Before planting, put down newspaper
so that any mess is easy to clear up.
You will need earth or potting
compost and some small pots.

Umbrella plant

When you are given a new plant
or cutting, ask how to look after it.
The Umbrella plant drinks lots of
water, because it lives in
marshy places in the wild.

However, many house plants die
from being given too much water.
So a plant may look sick
if it is too wet.

Busy Lizzie

Wandering Jew

Some plants need hardly any water
during the winter months
when they are not growing.
Some plants grow better if you
feed them when you water them
in the summer.

If you are not sure how to look after
one of your plants, borrow
a book about all the different
house plants from the library.
Why not ask for a plant book for a
birthday present.

When the earth
feels dry, it is
time to water
your Spider plant.

The Slipper flower
is an annual and
dies after it has
flowered.

You can start some plant cuttings in water
to make sure the roots are growing.

To grow an
Umbrella plant,
trim the leaf ends off
an 'Umbrella' and put
it down into water.

After a week
or so it should
start to grow
roots.

Plant it with
the umbrella
leaves and roots
in the earth.

A new plant
should start
growing.

The **Wandering Jew** can
also be grown from stem cuttings.
Keep them in water until
the roots start to grow.
Plant the rooted stems in
a flower pot.

Ask someone with a **Busy Lizzie** to give you a stem.
Keep it in water until the roots start to grow.

Plant the Busy Lizzie in a pot.
It should flower
a few weeks later.

After flowering, a **Spider plant** will grow small new plants at the end of its stems. Cut one off and put it in water until the roots grow. When they are about 2 cm long it is ready for planting.

Mustard and Cress will grow on
damp paper towels.
Read how to grow them on
the seed packet.
You can grow cress on cotton wool or
paper towels in an eggshell.
Draw a face on the eggshell
to go with its green hair.

It will be ready to cut
in about two weeks.
It tastes good when added
to sandwiches.

Chinese bean sprouts will grow on a damp bed of paper towels or cotton wool on a tray or dish.

Wash the Mung beans
under a cold tap
then soak them overnight.

Wash the beans again and spread them
on the damp bed. Don't make them too wet or
they will go mouldy.
Put the dish in a plastic bag and wrap newspaper
round to keep out the light. Check each day
to make sure the bed is damp.

After about a week
the bean sprouts will
be 2.5—3.5cm long
and ready to eat.

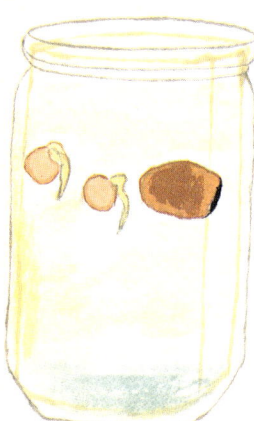

After a week
the peas
start to grow.

You can see how roots grow into the earth by planting dried **peas** or **broad beans** or **sweetcorn** in a jam jar with a tube of blotting paper to support them and keep them damp.

Keep a small amount of water in the bottom of the jar.

In four weeks the shoot grows up from the broad bean.

Pea after 10 days.

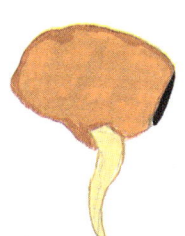

In 10 days the broad bean will start to grow too.

After four weeks the pea has grown leaves, and tendrils to help them to climb.

Avocado plants will start
growing in water too.
One may grow into a
house plant and last
for many years.

Put an avocado stone
in warm water and leave
in a warm place for two days.

Push four pins through
the skin of the stone and
rest them on the rim of the jar.

Not all avocado stones will
grow. Don't give up too soon,
as it may take six weeks for
it to start growing.

When the shoot and leaves
push through, plant it
in a flower pot.

Peanuts are fun too.
They need to be kept very warm
and wet. I put mine by a storage
heater. The polythene bag over the
pot helped to keep in the heat.

After flowering in the summer,
the peanut should grow the big
peanut seed shells. If you are
lucky it may plant the seeds itself
by pushing them into the ground.

Crack the shells of the
peanuts and plant them
still in their shells
in wet compost.

After five days or
so the root will
start to grow down
pushing the shell
upwards out of the earth.

A week later
green leaves
will sprout.

The peanut plant is an annual
and only lasts for one season.
But **fruit pips** will grow into small
trees which may last for many years.

Plant the pips in a flower pot.
Water them and cover with cling film
or a polythene bag until
they start to grow.

This lemon tree is
about six months old.

My peanut plant
after 3 weeks.

My orange pip
took four weeks
to start growing.

Acorns, conkers, sycamore and **ash seeds**
can all be planted in flower pots and
grown as house plants.
The leaves of these trees change
colour in the autumn.
It doesn't mean your tree has died.

If the trees get too big for the house,
plant them outside and after many years
they could grow into big trees.

Collect the seeds when they fall from
the trees in the autumn.
Most seeds grow better if they are
planted in the spring.
Keep them outside in damp sand
for the winter.

To stop animals eating
the seeds, put them
in a tin of sand.
Get someone to punch holes
in the tin to let air in.

You can grow an acorn
in water too. If the neck
of the bottle is too big,
a roll of plasticine or
blu-tack will stop the
acorn from falling in.

A glass container with a garden in it is called
a **Terrarium**. You can make one in a clean
glass mixing bowl, fish tank, or large glass bottle.
You will need:

Clean gravel   wash it in a sieve
by running water
through it.

Charcoal   chopped up small.
You can use barbecue charcoal
or buy it from a pet shop.

Potting compost

If you can't get your hand into your bottle or jar,
tie an old teaspoon to a long stick
to help reach the bottom and plant the plants.

Ask someone to help you choose small
slow-growing houseplants for your terrarium.

First put in the gravel, then a thin layer of charcoal. Add the potting compost and press down. Now plant your garden with tiny houseplants. Press them firmly into the compost. Remember your plants will grow, so don't make your garden too crowded.

Water the plants by running water down the sides of the jar, this will also wash the glass. Put the top back on the jar. It shouldn't need watering again. If it hasn't got a top, use a piece of cling film. If the glass clouds over, take the top off for a little while.

Maidenhair fern

Polka Dot

I made my garden in a large sweet jar.

These **cacti** are desert plants. They store water in their thick stems to use if it doesn't rain for a long time. They grow best on a sunny windowsill. In the summer, water them as soon as the earth in the top of the pots has dried out.

Prickly pear

Peanut cactus

Keep your cacti on a windowsill in a
cool room for the winter, and don't water
them until early spring.

Some grow baby cacti. These can
be taken off to start new plants.
Let them dry for a few days, then
plant them in small pots on their own.
To stop the spines getting in your fingers,
wear gloves when replanting your cacti.

Column
cactus

Tom Thumb
cactus

Some cacti
may flower
in the spring.

Crown
cactus

Easter
cactus

Christmas cactus and **Easter cactus** are really jungle cacti. In the wild they would be growing on rain forest trees, planting themselves between the branches.
Water them with rain water if possible, as they don't like hard tap water.

Christmas cactus

During the spring and summer, you can grow new plants from cuttings.
Take two or three pieces of stem and plant the bottom segment of each in potting compost.
Keep the compost damp.

Let the stems dry for a day or so before you plant them.

If you plant bulbs in early autumn they should start to flower soon after Christmas. Plant them in bulb fibre or earth. Try growing **Hyacinths** in water and watch their roots grow down. Keep your pots of bulbs in a cold dark cupboard until the shoots start to show.

This hyacinth is now ready to bring out of the cupboard. Long roots are growing down to the bottom of the jar. Its shoot is starting to grow too.

If the neck of the jar is too big for the bulb, make a roll of plasticine or blu-tack and stick it inside the rim of the jar.

Crocus corms and **snowdrops** grow best in the cold. Plant them in pots and leave them outside until the flower buds grow, then bring them indoors.

Yellow crocuses don't like flowering indoors. So plant a bowl of purple, mauve or white ones.

Hyacinth

Crocus

Snowdrop

If you touch the leaves of the
Touch-me-not or Sensitive plant
they will fold up and the stem
will droop downwards!
It will soon recover, but it may
stop closing up if you play with it
too often.